THE UTOPIAN COUNTRY

The answer to the five questions of Ezra Pound by Giacinto Auriti

"The utopian country" is a free translation of
"Guardiagrele: il paese dell'utopia" by Giacinto Auriti,
2002

The Utopian Country

Translation by ©Daniele Pace 2012

First Edition in English: February 2012
Second Edition in English: July 2013
First Edition in Italian September 2003

The book contemplates what Professor Auriti theorized and declare in the Rimini Conference in 1971 and wrote 10 years later on the book "The International Ordering of the Monetary System"

This book is focused only on the philosophy of the value and its induction.

The author Giacinto Auriti made this book available in Italian for free in PDF. The translator made the same on internet for a free PDF copy. Feel free to share it.

If you want buy the paperback to help the researcher Daniele Pace please visit: http://www.lulu.com/shop/giacinto-auriti/the-utopian-country/paperback/product-21105151.html

© **Cover by Sandra Internullo**

THE UTOPIAN COUNTRY
The answer to the five questions of Ezra Pound
by Giacinto Auriti

The Utopian Country

Table of Contents

Introduction..9
Translator's preface 13
The importance of Auriti and the legal definition of money [1].......15

THE UTOPIAN COUNTRY 21

Ezra Pound and Romanticism in the Twentieth Century.................23
Value is a relationship between phases of time..............................26
1-2 Money and circulation..29
3 – Credit 33
4 – Interest 35
5 – Usury...39
Conclusion...41

1) Notes on the philosophy of value 45
2) Why the Euro is an awkward currency? 51
3) The "colonial" currency 52
4) The outrageous falsehoods of scandals or the true scandal of falsehoods? 54
5) The reasons behind the "face off" between Industrial Confederation and the Unions. The malady of surplus value and flexibility..57
6) The "snag" in art. 107 of the Maastricht Treaty. Europe like Argentina? 59
7) Karl Marx was the first to denounce the giant scam. "Reducing taxes by eliminating the waste"???!!! 62
8) Monetary strategy during the FIAT crisis 65
9) "Descent of the Barbarians" 67
10) The chain letter and the sword of Damocles in the hands of the great usurers...69
11) Money as blood 71

12) The Euro as strong as the "Quota 90" Lira? 75

THE SOLUTION..**77**
BILL PROPOSAL for the "Popular Ownership of Money"
11th January 1995

13) Bill for the popular ownership of the Euro 79
THE BILL 83
Post Scriptum: Guardiagrele the Utopian Country........................85

*First edition in Italian: September 2002
by Giacinto Auriti. Faculty of Law, University of Teramo,
Italy*

The translator for a better understanding of this book has add a chapter from is book, **The Utopian Money**, published in 2012. The chapter, **The importance of Auriti and of the legal definition of money**, would put off the reader from the classical modern vision of the economy, according which economy is suppose to be like a science with an autonomous behaviour. This chapter added by the translator will explain to the reader why economy can not be a science and why must be regulated by the conventional law.

*"When Ben Dyson wrote on The Guardian the piece 'Money has been privatised by stealth' on November 2011 I understood that English reformers were going to the same direction revealed by Professor Auriti in 1971, when he discovery the **induced value of money** and propose the **Popular ownership of money**. To privatise is in fact a legal case, not an economic one, and money must be viewed by the jurisprudence as Auriti done long time ago. In November 2012 I understood that it was time to translate the works of Auriti in English, and this is the first one."*

Daniele Pace

The Utopian Country

Introduction

"I am a farmer who has exercised the hobby of a university professor"
Giacinto Auriti

Ezra Loomis Pound (Hailey, Idaho, 1885 - Venice 1972) and Giacinto Auriti (Guardiagrele 1923 – Rome 11 August 2006), the Poet and the farmer Lawyer. The American, who chose Italy as his adopted country and the Italian from the Abruzzo region. Apparently different characters, origin and culture, but are united by an indissoluble bond: the search for the truth at all costs.
Ezra Pound, an American poet, fascinated by the European culture, from the Middle Ages of "Padre Dante", where he discovers a universal reality to draw the inspiration for the "Pisan Cantos", (poem written during his imprisonment in the American concentration camp at Coltano in the Province of Pisa, where he was incarcerated in a cage). It was the price that he had to pay because of his love for Italy and having observed with interest at the awakening of Europe.
The poet felt the need of a renovation that was not restricted to a sterile exercise of rhetoric youth, but which constituted the foundation of a lived life and not a vegetated one: so inner cleansing, elimination of false myths of surrogate ideology of ideals: "As long as you have not cleared your thoughts within yourself, you can not communicate them to others. Until you do not put order within yourself, you cannot be element of order in the party".

Giacinto Auriti, developed a new philosophical theory in the meaning of the value as *"relationship between phases of time"* that would lead him to the discovery of the ***"induced value"*** of money.

The two personalities who never met, are united by a prophecy contained in verse 101-102 of "L'inferno", where the poet, after speaking of the she-wolf that kept him off his path, announcing the arrival of hound "that will cause her death with grief".

The "she-wolf" for Pound is the usury, against which he struggle for a new conception of life. Labour and usurer is the title of a collection of essays written after the Second World War, on the front page it reads *"Bellum cano perenne, between the usury and the man who wants do a good job"*. Pound realises that the money is not a commodity but the expression of an agreement, of a convention, for which the credit must be entrusted not to the banks but to the State, which shall guarantee its honestly by the work of its citizens. *"The treasure of a nation is its honesty"*, and in the "Cantos" it expresses the thought of usury: "With usury no man has a house of solid stone" / each block cut smooth and well fitting / that design might cover their face"
(Against usurer, Canto XLV).

Ezra Pound puts five questions to which no one has ever answered: money, credit, interest, usury and circulation.
Giacinto Auriti gives, in this essay, accurate answers. An ideal continuity that unites them in the school of economists heretic. Giacinto Auriti says: *"Who creates the value of currency is not who prints it but the people who accepts as a medium of payment"*, however, are the bankers, the big money-lenders who appropriate themselves of the monetary value, using it as a medium of domination and imposing to humanity the seigniorage of debt. Hence here is the brilliant solution to the problem. The popular ownership of money which returns to the people the stolen monetary value, that itself created. The hope is that governments have to manage money emission dividing the profits, as a right of citizenship to all citizens.

Introduction

The two intellectuals, the American poet, born from Quaker and Puritan parents, and the Lawyer from Abruzzo, conservative and Catholic, have both been gratuitously opposed by the culture of mass, plagiarized by the mystifying acceptance of the masters of usury, the money suppliers. Ezra Pound, in our opinion, has never emotionally detached from the rural America, but is fascinated by the creative and innovative force of war for the blood against gold, which creates new thriving cities where before the malaria, pestilence and death prospered.

Among the many followers of the Auriti's theories there are leftists, who by virtue of those theories they begin to hope for a future freed from seigniorage usury.

As the same Auriti points out, in Labour and usury Pound writes: *"On September 10th last year I passed along the Salaria Route, over the city of Fara Sabina, and after some time I entered the Republic of Utopia, a placid country distant from the present geography"*. In a footnote, Pound adds: *"I had written: "Utopia, a peaceful town lying eighty years East of the city Fara Sabina"*.

Since in this sentence matches a spatial and a temporal dimension, it must be evidenced that at East of the city of Fara Sabina is Guardiagrele, where SIMEC (Simboli Econometrici di Valore Indotto – Econometric Symbols of Induced Value) was founded, defined by monetarists as the Pound money. This system meant the money was owned by the bearer and not by the bank and was introduced eighty years after the birth of Fascism (1921- 22). And Guardiagrele is East of Fara Sabina. The Pound prophecy became true. It could be a sign of revenge for blood against gold.

On the side of SIMEC is shown an ancient phrase of the Abruzzo wisdom: *"Non bene pro toto libertas venditur auro"* (It is not a good thing to sell freedom for all the gold in the world) that echoes Pound's teaching: *"The treasure of a nation is its honesty."*

We begin to hope.........
Marino Solfanelli

The Utopian Country

Translated by Daniele Pace

Translator's preface

Professor Giacinto Auriti discovered the *induced value of money* and declared the *Popular Ownership of money* in 1971 at the Rimini Conference, and then he wrote *The International Ordering of Monetary System* in 1981. Since that date the monetary system is changed again but the Auriti's theory is still the final solution at the problem because sees the money from a different point of view, that one of the jurisprudence, thus solving the problem as now, when commercial banks create the 97% of the money out of nothing by the credit as it will be explained in the chapter add to this book by the translator, directly from is book *The Utopian Money.* [a]

This chapter, *The importance Auriti and of the legal definition of money,* would put off the reader from the classical modern vision of the economy, according which economy is suppose to be like a science with an autonomous behaviour. This chapter added by the translator will explain to the reader why economy can not be a science and why must be regulated by the conventional law.

The giant mistake in thinking economy as a science put that above the society, and them as master of the humankind and like an instrument. But because economy and money are produced by the society, they must be under that, functioning for the wealth and not for the profit. The *induced value* and the *Popular ownership of money* led in the past some honest senators to present for three times a proposal bill for giving the ownership of money to the citizenship.

To understand this book it is necessary know that the Italian Central Bank was half public since the fascist government provided to create three important public banks in 1933, which held a large part of

The Utopian Country

Bank of Italy.
However it became totally private since 1994, after the left party privatised it to pay the national debt.
Giacinto Auriti and Ezra Pound were born in 1923 and in 1885, a time when all Central Banks of the world were privates and only the Italian and German banks, were respectively public or semi-public. That represented a great change in the world for the time, and attracted sympathy from many people who saw, even by mean of a dictatorship, a way to liberate the nations from the debt.
At the time the people was very conscious about the problem and it was living the great depression which seems coming back today.
Professor Auriti, died in 2006, studied for 35 years the monetary system, and published this book in 2002, after many works about the money since 1960. In the meantime professor Auriti has complained at the Italian Tribunal against the Bank of Italy, for fraud, criminal association and many other crimes. In collaboration with the University of Teramo he forced the Bank to admit his responsibility in front to the tribunal and he inspired in the 90's some bill for a monetary reform never passed by the parliament.
The theory proposed by Professor Auriti could today be applied to the whole banking system because it explains why the currency has a value and why it cannot be issued by the banks instead of the government, at any level.
This theory, not completed yet to include the new facts happened in the meantime, open the mind to a new economy, where the debt towards the banking system is abolished, both if it is towards Central Banks or towards the commercial banks.
This theory could be seen as a utopia, but is from dreams that were born the social achievements of the twentieth century.
It is not just an improvement of the actual banking system, but an authentic economic revolution which will promote a new the economy.

Daniele Pace

The importance of Auriti and the legal definition of money [1]

Professor Giacinto Auriti was not a monetarist, but a jurist of international law who wrote about the money, and this may seem strange to those who would like to understand how run the monetary system and the debt.

In reality, Auriti has made a fundamental contribution to the understanding of money precisely by virtue of the fact that analysed the monetary field from a legal point of view and not economic, and in this way doing to answer the fundamental questions that monetarists and economic schools were not able to give a definitive answer over the centuries.

This is because they had not understood what was the true nature and function of money, ignoring Aristotle. When we went out, with Auriti, of the strictly economic analysis to join the field of law, the only one able to define in its entirety the essence of money, the definition immediately seemed clear.

The money should be seen as a legal point of view for several reasons. If after centuries did not find answers in economic matters it is because that field is not the most comprehensive and suitable for this response, as the monetary phenomenology is not a case purely economic but also involves the legal, sociological, philosophical and psychological one, observing both behaviour over the centuries, that its origin.

The pure economic matters so far it has managed to define only its operation in the financial markets as a commodity, but could not justify the ownership and its destructive nature related to issue and debt.

Auriti studied the money for 35 years, observing the behaviour both in the value that in the symbol, placing a fundamental question that with the repeal of the Bretton Woods showed clearly the legal nature of the money: what gives value to money.
If the practice of banking fractional reserve could not reveal this nature, because masked and always interpreted as a fraud at first, and then as a legal banking practice, the end of Bretton Woods and the subsequent declaration of trustworthy value of money, made clear the need to apply the *"circularity of science", thus when you can not explain a phenomenon in the scientific category in which it occurs, should be changed to a different category by applying the scientific principle by analogy* [2].
The new definition of value for money, given by the same banking system, as a trustworthy value, that public confidence in the currency, already requires a reflection, as confidence is certainly not a purely economic matter, but a social and psychological phenomenon to be analysed according to the rules of sociology and psychology.
So if, for the same declaration of the international bankers, the value is based on trust, and currently the financing of the EU members through the sale of government securities, depends on the confidence of financial markets, the monetary part falls in the fields different, mentioned above, and the money must be submitted to their analysis and to a law, other than the purely economic and banking one, which also includes compliance with the legal rules that, in the twentieth century, have embraced the demands posed by these matters, contemplating many laws derived from these studies.
The *circularity of science* is already widely applied in those areas where specific legislation has proved ineffective. To cite just one recent example we can mention the new regulations regarding the bullying at work, which certainly do not cover only the problems closely related to the employment law, but are dictated also by social

and psychological mechanisms resulting from abuse and harassment also very important findings in health such as depression or social exclusion and how that, when recognized, the law gives big payouts. In the example of bullying we do not have an exclusive employment legislation, but the involvement of sociologists, psychologists and doctors, for its definition and preparation, and application of a law that is able to address the problem.

Starting right from this example it is clear that the money and the economy, which are pure social phenomena, must be regulated by the conventional law, having not independent existence.

Similarly, the same principles of *circularity* should be applied to the problem of money, now more evident than ever, to understand its functioning abnormally already proven over the centuries, and especially its definition, given by the same creators of money, of trustworthy value.
Over the centuries, the money had already been shown to have a precise definition of its material value, being once gold, once silver, once wood (in Tally Sticks), once tea (in the east) and many other forms and materials gradually assumed in different societies and eras.
With the repeal of Bretton Woods, and the final shape and material that cost nothing, the money has clearly placed the question of the nature of its essence.
The answer provided by the banking system, it did more than reiterate the need for a different approach to the monetary system, confirming to the above, the legal, sociological, philosophical and psychological essence, while the economy it can only explain the operation and adjust the issuing.

The importance of the Auriti's works is therefore essential to give a definitive answer to the concept of money in the value. Once we have defined the real essence of money and its value, we can not run into the errors of the past, and the money will go back to being an instrument of society and not its master.

What may seem abstruse in the Auriti's works and an end in itself, actually represents the liberation of humanity from the slavery of money and his addiction. It is the liberation of humanity from the yoke of usurers and the new slavers financial, to achieve a new world, fair, supportive and free of imbalances, where money is no longer a problem and the man will be central and not marginal.

Distinguishing between symbol and value for money, Auriti has identified the fields to define money, thus being able to give legal status to its definition, and therefore assigning the ownership discovering the source of value, by applying the *circularity of sciences*, he has defined both the measure of the value that the value of the measure.

The result is the **Popular Ownership of the Money** and its **induced value**, two fundamental concepts that redefine the money in its purest form.

If the theory can certainly seem complicated due to the hostility that often accompanies the understanding of fields embraced for the definition of money, the practice in real and concrete life results in a disarming simplicity even for its application.

Many, after reading Auriti, fail to see in reality the usefulness of his discovery on the *Induced Value* and the *Ownership of money*, not by understanding both the practical and legal effects.

In its practical and legal application, thanks to the juridical basis provided by Auriti, the money created and issued with a debt will be illegal.

The money should instead be legally issued and distributed free of charge without interest to all those who create value through the work, the production and circulation.

The banks will not be able to create money out of nothing and charging it with interests and they can carry out only function of deposit and borrowing of existing money as it was in their original functions when the goldsmiths guarded the gold of investors for a fee. This will resize the banking system by returning the production and the work of man at the centre of the economy, where money is only the measure of value and the value of the measure.

In the phrase of Auriti: *"As each unit of measure is a convention and every convention is a legal case, money is a legal case. Therefore, the raw material to manufacture currency is the same as that used to produce legal case: form and spiritual reality that symbol and Monetary Convention"*, **[2]** there is contained all the cultural revolution that would come from a deep consciousness of the nature of money.

Spirituality and deep consciousness of society are essential to understanding the monetary phenomenon, while the economic mechanisms can only adjust the operation so that it does not create problems of poor service.

The money can not be refused, nor by the State, nor by the banks, to the society as belonging to the same society, and lenders may charge a maximum production costs, now zero, which makes the banking system itself useless.

[1] Daniele Pace, The Utopian Money, *The Importance of Auriti and the legal value of money*, pag 287 (http://www.lulu.com/shop/daniele-pace/the-utopian-money/paperback/product-21398422.html)

[2] Giacinto Auriti, The Utopian Country, *Money and the circulation*

The Utopian Country

THE UTOPIAN COUNTRY

The answer to the five questions of Ezra Pound by Giacinto Auriti

©Translated by Daniele Pace 2012

The Utopian Country

Ezra Pound and Romanticism in the Twentieth Century

"The nineteenth century, the infamous century of usury..." **(1)**; *I went to sleep under the Sabine stars, (...) amazed for the difference between the world of the twentieth century and that one of serenity..."* **(2)**.
With these two lapidary sentences, Pound expresses the causal link between two centuries of history: *post hoc ergo propter hoc* (after this therefore because of this). It is the advent of usurocrazy the cause of anxiety that characterizes the spiritual climate of our time. It is not a case that in the language of American merchant practice usury is defined by the term "danger". The danger is incompatible with serenity.

As Pound understood: *"In the century of usury all nations have become poor because they were indebted for a value equal to all their money since 1694, year that the Bank of England was established"*.

These few words show the magnitude of intuition of Pound. The whole culture of the twentieth century is filled with romanticism. You feel, you suffer the great problems that afflict the generation: the philosophical and scientific knowledge to solve them is missing.

"What has been lacking in Italy, especially among practical people, industrialists, large or small, among the merchants and not only

among the small traders, it is the vision of process of usury. The knowledge of the relationship, and the relationships among business, the management of manufacturing or commercial company, and the world monetary system, operating not with a short deadline, not in periods of three months or three years, but in the long run over centuries and half- centuries, always with the same purpose: to gain profit. And always with the same mechanisms, that is creating debts to take advantage of the interests, and monopolies to vary the price of everything, including price the various units of the different currencies of different nations" **(3)**.

Pound has pointed out that money is the great gap of the Roman Christian cultural tradition. While declaring itself Fascist, it highlights the cultural limitations of Fascism, common to all Romantic movements of the twentieth century. Romanticism means to feel the problems of their own generation with blood and not with the brain.

With humbleness equal to his love for the truth, he says: "**...we ask what is money, credit, interest, usury".**

"Before discussing a monetary policy, a monetary reform, a monetary revolution, we must be very sure of the nature of money.

"The enemy is ignorance (ours). At the beginning of the nineteenth century John Adams (pater patriae) saw the defects and errors of the U.S. government derived not so much from the corruption of staff, but because of ignorance of money, credit, and their circulation."

"We are at the same point" **(4)**.

Today we again ask ourselves. Are we at the same point?
We think not. We are in fact now in a position to be able to give a complete answer to the five questions posed by Pound: *"What is the money, credit, interest, usury, (...) and circulation"*.

We believe that answering these five questions, it will fill the cultural gap that caused the collapse of the old Catholic monarchies of Europe and the defeat of romanticism in the 900. For this purpose it seems essential to make a brief introduction to define the value and distinguish between physiology and pathology of judgements in the value.

(1) Ezra Pound, Labour and usury, Milan 1972, p. 25.
(2) E. Pound, op. Cit., p.
(3) E. Pound, op. Cit., p. 54.
(4) E. Pound, op. Cit., p. 20.

Value is a relationship between phases of time...

... thus for example, a pen has value because it is expected to write, the knife has value because it is expected to cut, money has value because you expected to buy. The value is therefore the relationship between the time of the prediction and the foreseen time.

As Kant said: Because time is the "I" that stands as reality as the capacity in place to observe, predict and remember - and the "I present" in its vital continuity is the constant of time, it explained why, it is not conceivable time without life, that is, "value without life", as there is no wealth in a world of dead.

The error of the romantic schools is mainly due to the fact that they conceived the values as properties of the material, that is as a dimension of space. Space coincides only with the present: all the rest is time.
Therefore, Pound, even if he recognised the problem he was unable to resolve it because the economic culture ignored (and still ignores it) the phenomenon of the forecast activities in which the same judgement of value is achieved.

This cultural landmark is denounced by Pound in a significant sentence: "... I approve with relief the tendency of F. Ritter to speak about money not in terms of "finance" and "economy" but in terms of wheat and fertilizer" **(5)**. The expression is a significant example of romantic culture of the twentieth century: noble and ingenious in

Value is a relationship between phases of time...

identifying and criticizing the evil tyranny of usury, but unable to indicate constructive remedies. If Ritter's theory was true there would be no difference between bartering and trading. Only after the discovery of the induced value is it possible differentiate between the value of the measurement (money) from the value measured (wheat and fertilizer).

Once shown that the value is a relationship between phases of time, we have to separate instrumental phase related to the object (example the pen) and the hedonistic one related to the subject (example write with the pen).

This distinction between objective and subjective moment in which you realize that the physiology of value, based of course on the dualistic conception of the philosophy of knowledge (Aristotelian-Thomistic), which distinguishes the object from the subject.

Since the past and the future do not coincide with the "I" present (which is the constant of time) they are the object of memory and the expectation that is the object of the judgement value.

When the judgement value is built on the philosophical basis of the Hegelian monism (in which it confuses the object with the subject for the reduction of reality to the idea of reality in the idealism), it is immanent the instrumental objective moment with the hedonistic subjective one, with the result of personifying the instrument. Thus the concept was born of a society without human content, the legal ghost that has characterized the advent of capitalism, of which usury intuited by Pound, is constitutive and an essential part.

With confusion between the instrumental or functional moment (prerogative of the organ) and the hedonistic time (prerogative of the social collectivity) it was founded, in fact, the great cultural disease of the organic representation of the hedonistic moment of value. As if

The Utopian Country

to say - referring at the apologue of Menenio Agrippa - while the people assume the role of hunger, the government assume the role of eating in representation of the people.

The property (including also that of money) – which is the enjoyment of the goods legally protected and then belonging to the second stage of the time of value – is taken from the human person and given to the legal ghosts. The instrumental subjectivity, operational tools of capitalism, have become the screens of large mangers. Constitutional state, socialist state, anonymous societies, state agency, bank, corporation, etc.. are all concepts of a society without human content, or rather the instruments that have distorted the ethical basis of the traditional organic society. No coincidence that all banks are "Ltd companies".

Since it is impossible and absurd to serve an instrument, the rule of serving typical for the organic society has been replaced by that of serving yourself typical of the instrumental subjectivity.
The principle of "it is convenient to be fair" was subsequently replaced by the principle "it is right what is convenient". No coincidence that the phenomenon of Tangentopoli [a] is not only a statistical expression for increasing in political crime, but demonstrates, in its impotence, the sign of the declining times that we are experiencing.
In these circumstances we answer the five questions of Ezra Pound.

---

(5) E. Pound, Labour and Usury, p. 56.
[a] *Tangentopoli* (sometimes translated as "bribesville") is a term which was coined to describe pervasive corruption in the Italian political system exposed in the 1992, (http://en.wikipedia.org/wiki/Tangentopoli)

1-2 Money and circulation

Money was exhaustively defined by Aristotle as a measure of value.
In each sentence there are always two meanings: one explicit and one implicit. The limit of monetarists lies in the fact that they are limited to considering only the explicit meaning of the Aristotle's definition, *"the measure of value"* and ignore the implicit *"value of the measure"*. Each unit of measure has, in fact, necessarily, the corresponding quality to what needs to be measured.
As the meter has the quality of the length because it measures the length, money has the quality of value because it measures the value. Thus money is not only the *measure of value*, but it is also the *value of the measure* that is the **purchasing power**.

Since each unit of value is a convention, and each convention is a legal case, money is a legal case.
Therefore, the raw material to manufacture currency is the same used to produce the same legal categories: form and spiritual reality that is the symbol and Monetary Convention.

In brief, the symbol acquires monetary value simply because it has been agreed upon. Predicting the behaviour of others as a condition of your own, induces others to accept money for goods because in turn it will give you money for goods.

The birth of monetary value, even in the symbol that costs nothing **(6)**, led Pythagoras to define the monetary value as the "magic of the number". As number it was intended the measure because each measure is a numeric expression: such is true as normally we talk about "units" of measurement.

To explain the mystery of the "magic of the number" we have applied the fundamental principle of the *"circularity of sciences"* so, when a phenomenon in the scientific category in which it occurs cannot be explained, it should be explained in a different scientific category, applying the principle by analogy. With this method we found the legal induction using the experience of physical induction. As the dynamo turns mechanical energy into electricity, so money transforms the value of a convention that is a spiritual reality, in a true object subject to possession.

The time is objectified by induction in a more intense way than is in other legal cases. While normally the instrumentality of any rule is unique in the typical *"normative prediction"*, the function of money is not restricted only to a conventional measuring (i.e. legislation) for the value of economic goods, but is itself object of trade because it incorporates the *"value of the measure"* by *"legal induction"*.

In the monetary case, the formal element of the symbol (monetary) is not only intended to demonstrate the convention, but giving to the bearer the prediction to be able *"to buy"*, the power to purchase, incorporates the "value of the measure" and thus becomes a new possession, completely independent and different from those measured, so much so that it constitutes consideration in the exchange negotiation of the sale.

This argument could not be considered by Pound because he did not know that the value is *"time"* and not *"space"*, in other words prediction and not commodities.
As in the dynamo, the alternating rotation between positive and negative poles causes the electromagnetic field to generate electricity, the monetary convention in the succession of the phases

1-2 Money and circulation

of the circulation of money in its own and others hands, results similarly to the alternation of the "'I" with the "not I", of mine with yours, that generates, by legal induction, the monetary value.

As in the physical induction electrical power happens when the rotation of the dynamo begins, similarly it birth the monetary value at the moment of issuing in the hands of who accept because it foresees the circulation into the legal induction.

As in the dynamo, when the speed of rotation is faster it increases the amount of electricity, thus increasing the velocity of the monetary circulation it increases the value induced, in other words the purchasing power.

On this principle the investment banks create unlimited quantities of value by giving the bank deposits the speed of light transferring them from one continent to another with the electronic pulses of computers. The phenomenon has been described by the Governor of the Bank of Italy, as "transnational deposit that avoids the control of the central banks". Since the induced value is caused by the circulation of money, similar to electricity caused by the dynamo rotation, lacking the scientific awareness of the phenomenon, the governor Fazio, to express the concept, linked the word "deposit" that has a static meaning, to the term "transnational" that has a dynamic meaning. Therefore, he proposed an irrational definition of the induced value because it is expressed with two terms mutually incompatible.

In conclusion, money is not only the product of a convention, but a conventional activity that, in its continuity, creates the "purchasing power" by induction in a case of sociology juridical.
Money that does not circulate is a mere symbol, not money.
The symbol of money can become all possible forms of legal categories. As the red and green traffic lights follow the form of a

legal norm, because they allow and prohibit the transit, *thus the symbol of money can be achieved, by convention, in the light of the computer.*

To explain the difference between jurisprudence and sociology juridical it only requires an elementary example: the *"purchase agreement"* is a legal case; *"buyer and seller bound by the contract"* is a case of legal sociology. It is in this second case that arises and exists in its continuity, the *induced value*.

As electricity is caused by the rotation that alternates positive and negative poles of the generating elements, as the "I" and the "other", the "I" and the "not I", are the "legal poles" in which the induced value is born.
As electricity does not born if the generator does not run, so the monetary value does not arise if the money does not circulate in the negotiating business market.
Money is jurisprudence that lives.

---

(6) Paper money created at pure printing cost.

3 – Credit

Credit has a corresponding value to the performance that is object of the credit. Money has a corresponding value to the total numerical unit of measure of the value that it represents. It is a pure legal value caused by social convention both in its essence than in its amount.

The credit, as for example the bill of exchange, is extinguished by payment. Money continues to circulate after each transaction because, as every unit of measure, it is a commodity with repeatable utility.

The monetary schools of today, ignoring the distinction between value of credit and induced credit, have defined money as the absurd formula of *"debt and / or junk debit"* to justify the existence and its repeated use. The result was an absurd statement placed on the banknotes (e.g. Thousand Lira payable to the bearer on demand. Signed by The Governor of the Bank of Italy) conceived as a false *bill of exchange*.

Since the value of the credit is given by its possibility to be payable, this money should have no value for us since it should be indifferent if we have or not have it in ours pockets.

The Monetary Agreement is so much more important than the language, that the indenture declaration on the banknote imposes even here an incompatible interpretation with the literal one. In fact, everyone knows, that the banknote, even though it is a false bill of exchange, it is *real money*.

Only on this basis can it be explained why Mr. Paterson founded the Bank of England in 1694 on the rule to lend the bank's (false) bill of exchange **[a]** instead of gold.

Since the value of the bill of exchange is given by the promise of the debtor, masquerading the banknotes under the appearance of a bill of exchange, the Governor claimed the right to the issuance of money that he had appropriated, because at the moment of its issuance he was lending it. *And this is the prerogative of the owner.*

Thus, the governor is the false debtor, but the true owner of money. In this way money born as the ownership of the banks that issues it, just lending it to citizens. Instead money should be the ownership of the citizens and be credited to them as an *Income of citizenship*.

The bank is therefore a criminal association which masquerades its crimes as a deal for its victims.

Once we have realised that money is a false bill of exchange, it is explained why the Central Bank accounts for the money issued as deficit **[b]**, falsifying the financial statements.

---

[a] As many others Auriti sees the banknotes, which are promissory notes, as well as false bills of exchange issued by the banks and believed money by the citizenship because bank promise with them the gold which does not have any more as reserve of the same notes, instead of which gold Auriti placed the induced value and the prediction of value created by the social convention.

[b] Most of the central banks account as liability the notes in circulation, hiding in this way most of the profit for seigniorage to transfer to the Treasury.

4 – Interest

Interest is the price paid for using money. By analogy we can say it is like a tenant who's paying the rent to the owner for the use of the apartment. The difference is that while in the rented house property remains in the hands of the landlord, in the rented money, that is a loan, the property passes into the hands of the tenant (the debtor) because essentially the enjoyment of having money is that it is spendable, being able to transfer the *property* at the time of purchase.

Closely related to the topic of interest is the rarity of money. In fact, the amount of interest is functionally connected to its rarity. Up until today no school has been able to give a valid scientific justification to the limit of its rarity on which to schedule its issuance. This is the reason why there is no possibility to set up a criteria of technical discretionary to justify and regulate scientifically the "must be" of the monetary function.

This gap in monetary science finds its significant expression in reply given by President Einaudi to those who asked him what was the law of rarity: *"The rarity of gold has been replaced by the wisdom of the governors".*

These words, in their evident absurdity, are the symptoms of well-established habit in practice to attribute to the governor of the central bank not an organic function, as it should be, but the absolute, uncontrollable and irrevocable discretion because they are carried out by a "Wise" par excellence, even if in violation of criminal laws.

Therefore, the solution to the problem is only possible if you understand that money must be rare because it measures the value of economic goods because they are rare, i.e. limited in the amount compared to the level of need. Since each unit must have the matching quality to what it should measure, as the meter has the quality of length because it measures length, money must have the quality of rarity because rare are the assets of which the value is measured.

When money was gold, the major flaw was the stiff and uncontrollable rareness. With the advent of the nominal money, the rarity has been programmed not according to the objectives of social interests, but those of the usury.

In other words, given that the market price is not only the index of the value of goods, but also the point of saturation of the market - thus the market is saturated when the price tends to coincide with the costs of production - only when this trend occurs, should it desist from both the production of goods and the issuance of currency.

This standardization of the market is possible only if the money is declared from the issuance, **ownership of the bearer** and **without reserve**. When it is issued on loan and with reserve, the market is dominated by the usury for two reasons:

a) because, upon issuance, it was born as property of the bank which issues it only in lending it, i.e. charging a *debt not due* to the market to which bankers can claim the return arbitrarily in times and quantities determined by the unchallengeable Governor of the Central Bank (a limited private company with a profitable aim);

b) because, once it has been shown that money has an induced and not credit value, the reserve serves only as a pretext to justify a limited amount of money to be issued (allegedly arbitrarily established) on that one of the reserve.

This is why the Central Bank, at the moment that it issues money, to maintain control of the monetary values created by the citizens (and it should therefore be credited to them), issues currency only by a loan thus as debt-money, in the most gigantic scam of all times. The enormous usury has in this way transformed the population of owners in debtors of its own money.

Only on this basis it is explained the note that appeared on Hazard Circular in 1862, cited by Pound: *"The great debt that the capitalists will see to it is made out of the war, must be used as a means to control the volume of money. To accomplish this the bonds must be used as a banking basis. We are now waiting for the Secretary of the Treasury to make this recommendation to Congress. It will not do to allow the Greenback, as it is called, to circulate as money any length of time, as we cannot control that. But we can control the bonds and through them the bank issues."* **(7)**.

Pound is right when he says: *"The usurers cause wars to create debts"* **(8)**. Since we know that the same money today is a debt because it is issued by central banks only as a loan, Pound's phrase should be completed this way: *"to pay others debts for a chronic and inescapable insolvency"*.

Today we have proof that the war is not only a medium to preserve and increase the debt (not due), but to avoid the extinction of debt (with state notes), even murder is included. Recently the journal *"Chiesa Viva"* **(9)** under the title "The Assassination of John F. Kennedy" has documented the truth about the historic crime. After the assassination of the President, Vice President JB Johnson, just after taking the position of President, orders the withdrawal of all the notes printed by Kennedy with his Executive Order 11110 of June 4, 1963. These notes did no longer show the writing "FEDERAL

RESERVE NOTE", but "UNITED STATES NOTE "(!!!) as it is apparent from the two images reproduced in the article. So Kennedy understood that the hegemony of usury was based on the rule born with the central bank, "to issue currency lending it to the nations collectivity" that, by creating the value with the acceptance, it must, instead be owned right from the moment of its issuance.

That is why everybody can lend money, except who issues it.

Issuing currency by lending it is the seigniorage of the big usury, which was born in 1694 with the Bank of England, as reported by Pound "..*a criminal association..*" **(10)**.

Pound, however, made a mistake when, commenting the words of Paterson, limiting usury to 60%. The famous sentence of William Paterson, founder of the Bank of England was: *"The Bank benefits from the interest of all money created out of nothing"* **(11)**, which appears unscrupulously honest, in fact it hides the most important part of the truth because it is not true that the bank is enriched only by interest, but also and first of all by the same money, of which the value - as we have seen - is not created by the bank, but by the community.
So the cost of money is not only 60%, but also an additional 200% because a credit is transformed (+100%) in a debt (-100%) without compensation!
The charity of banks is stronger than the Christian one.
The Christian charity teaches us to forgive debts. The bank's charity teaches even to pay the debtors. The central bank lends the amount which then cashes in as a creditor collects its own debts.

(7) E. Pound, Labour and usury, p. 14.
(8) E. Pound, Labour and usury, p. 14.
(9) Chiesa Viva, No 338, Brescia, April 2002, p. 15.
(10) E. Pound, Labour and usury, p. 10.
(11) E. Pound, Labour and usury, p. 19.

5 – Usury

The usury sensed by Pound is the seigniorage.

You cannot understand why Pound declared himself fascist if you do not start from the Mussolini's fundamental message: "*The war of blood against gold*". Furthermore, you cannot understand this message if we do not start from the fundamental concept of "*ethical state*" in which Catholicism is the "*Religion of the State*".
The absolute incompatibility between ethical and democratic state is in the fact that the foundation is the "*thirst for justice*", because ethic is a variant in which the law of numbers (the will of the majority) is, by its nature, neutral and modifiable with cultural strategies of domination (by the mass media).

The most important phenomenon, that took place with the French Revolution, was not the Constitution, but the central bank with the simultaneous replacement of the gold coin with the nominal money. This was not a simple change in the commodity structure of the symbol, but the substitution of a legal case with another. When money was gold, the bearer was its owner, but with the nominal money, it has become unwittingly debtor. All the nominal money is issued by central banks and then lending it: therefore all the money in circulation is charged with a debt towards the central banks.

Levering on the conditioned reflex caused by the secular habit of always giving a consideration for money, central banks have led all the people of the world to accept their own currency when issued, with the equivalent of a debt, i.e. a loan; in the biggest scam of all time, which went unnoticed because it was too obvious. So if someone wanted to pay a debt of money with money, it was as if a debt was being paid with another debt. In the long run he was forced to pay a debt not due, with his own capital and income of his work.

This is the *seigniorage* of the great usury with which man is placed at a rank lower than a beast. In fact, a beast has no property, but has no debt either. The *money-debt (nominal)* is the masterpiece of Satan. Usually the rule is that there are no good or bad medium, but just how good or bad they are used. With the money-debt who accepts it is cheated, just for the fact that accepts it, because he is expropriated and in debt by the fact that he borrows the his own money for which he creates the value in accepting it and in the meantime he appropriates himself a debt because he accepts the loan once issued. This not due debt, born, as we see, with an initial cost of 200% circulates in the *anguish of the inevitable insolvency.* It is the high-usury born with the sterling and the Bank of England in 1694.

The evidence for this is that once people worked for a profit, today they work to pay debts. Suicide by foreclosure has become a social disease that has no precedents in history: Pound was right "... *worse than plague is usury...*". The expression he proposed of "usurocracy" shakes the foundations of the *communis opinio* (common opinion) which placed the state of law of the liberal school, in the Olympus of the untouchable and final concepts. *"To Liberals (which are not all money- lenders) we ask: why are money lenders all Liberals? "* **(12)**

The fact that now the politician – as Pound said – the "banker's waiter", obviously emerges the consideration that if you compare the Governor of Central Bank and the PM of Government, the first may grant or deny to lend all the money he wants, the second can only ask or not ask, only for a loan. It is therefore obvious that the second is the *waiter of the first*, but not because he has a servile spirit, but because the rules of the game do not allow otherwise.

(12) E. Pound, op. Cit., p. 15.

Conclusion

In conclusion, the solution of the problems posed by Pound to the attention of the World is an action of recovery, in favour of every population, the ownership of their currency.

The Bank of England's monetary revolution has transformed the money-property of the bearer (gold) in the nominal money (debt for the bearer and property for the bank).

The counter-revolution must transform the money-debt in money-property of the bearer (not by the bank), without reserve (like gold), with a symbol of no cost (like paper).

Only in this way will it be possible restore the dignity juridical to every Man and release him from the anxiety of the inevitable insolvency of debts not due, allowing the people to finally live a new age on a human dimension.

The reader is not surprised by our admission that he had derived our answers from Pound's teaching, because Pound did not only give us the intuition of the monetary truth (the induced value of money), but also and above all, the great ethic in the research of the truth at all costs.

The Utopian Country

Conclusion

Contributions on Money

The Utopian Country

1) Notes on the philosophy of value

Space coincides only with the present, all the rest is time.

All schools of social and economic sciences have found it impossible to carry out a serious investigation because they lack the scientific assumptions of philosophy of value absolutely essential for an understanding and definition of the object of their search.

Since all serious scientific process, free from the banal and free constructions of empirical pragmatism, moves from the clarification of an initial postulate whose truthfulness, which can only be established and not proven, we assume the hypothesise that value is a relation between phases of time. Like the pen has a value because it is expected to write, the knife has the same value because it is expected to cut and money has value because is expected to buy.
Therefore, the value is the relationship between the time of its expectation and the foreseen time.

Given that time is the "*I*" that arises as a reality, capable in the act of remembering, observing and predicting, it might seem, at a first glance, that there is not an objective dimension of time because it coincides with "*the I thinking*". However, we realize that there is an objective time, as long as we take in consideration the fundamental hermeneutic principle of clarification of the observation point of the phenomenal reality. Since the constant of time is the present that is the I thinking in its vital continuity, the observation point of reality is the I present himself. The moment remembered and that one foreseen are not, obviously, the present: they are time thought and not time thinking. The objective reality of the present is space. Space in fact coincides only with the present. All the rest is time. The I present of the monetary time is the bearer of the money that is the point of observation that allows the objective spatial evaluation (which is the possession of the symbol) and the temporal evaluation (which is the expectation of being able to buy).

So, when the monetarists claim to define the value as a property of material – e.g. the intrinsic value of gold as a property of the metal – they fall into the irremediable mistake of considering the value in the dimension of space and since we have shown that the value is always a prediction that is a dimension of time, it falls in the absurd pretension of going in search of value where there is none. Also gold has value by convention, that is, for the prediction of acceptance of others as a condition of its acceptance as a measure of value and the value of the measure. Everyone is in fact willing to accept money against goods that in turn is expected to give money against goods. Even for gold, traditionally used as a currency symbol, the phenomenon of legal induction is verified. Gold, like every currency, even if it consists of symbols that have no cost, is a legal case because is a purely conventional value.

That said, it is clear that the raw material which manufactures money is the same needed to make a legal case i.e. form and spiritual reality, that is symbol and monetary convention. Because of the possible forms of the jurisprudence: written, spoken, behaviour (in the case of commodity money whose value was established for the constant repetition of the conclusive behaviour of acceptance), advertisement and light (such as green and red traffic lights are a form of "*should be*" legal, thus the lights of the computers have become "*monetary symbols*"), are also possible forms of money.

Only on this basis can place the fundamental distinction between *physiology* and *pathology* of the value as a foundation of all

1) Notes on the philosophy of value

scientific categories in which the researcher must have full knowledge that his cognitive ability is normal in the organic and contextual coordination of temporal and spatial dimension.

The judgement of the value is normal only if we distinguish the instrumental objective moment from the hedonistic subjective one. This means that the judgement of the value is normal only if it is based on a dualistic conception of the philosophy of the knowledge that distinguishes between subject and object.

The instrumental moment is the objective moment of the value because it is the objective moment of the time. The hedonistic moment is the subjective moment of the value because it is the subjective moment of time. Which always coincides with the present, that is, the I thinking.

The judgement of the value is abnormal when the instrumental moment is confused with the hedonistic one, in other words, when pursuant to the monist conception of the philosophy of knowledge, which reduces reality to the idea of reality, confuses the object with the subject and therefore the instrumental moment, the objective with the hedonistic one, which is subjective.

The macroscopic consequence of this deformation of the judgement of the value is the phenomenon of the personification of the instrument that has determined in the corporate law the overwhelming cultural disease of the instrumental subjectivity for which the society is not regarded as a set of members linked by the organic relationship of the members, but as a concept without human content: a true **legal ghost**.

The real and unspeakable purpose of the cultural strategy that has designed and implemented the phenomenon of the instrumental subjectivity, was to allow exploiting companies the monstrous organic representation of the hedonistic moment of value, which is capitalism. In other words, while the people assumes the function of being hungry, the government assumes the function of eating, representing the people. The historical experience of Hegelian rationalism has taught us that Monism has been exploited to confuse the object with the subject, i.e. the *"I"* with the *"not I"*, that is the *"I"* with *"you"* and *"mine"* with *"yours"*, because *"yours"* can become mine. That is why Hegel is the philosopher of capitalism.

Reduced the concept of society as an instrument, i.e. a concept without a human content, the inevitable consequence has been the replacement of the rule of *"to serve yourself"* to that one *"to serve"* (typical of the organic society and of natural jurisprudence) because it is ridiculous to think that you can serve an instrument. Consequently, natural ethic has been replaced by *it is convenient to be right, with the economic ethic what is convenient is right*.

Here, the social interest cannot coincide with those of the members because the "instrumental society" are not the *"members"*.
Under the mask of social interest hides the social interest of a legal ghost which is nothing else than a cover up for the large manger of the instrumental society. That is why with the advent of instrumental subjectivity, only times of decadence have lived and necessarily live because the *"worse"* rules the world. In fact, reduced the reality to the I thinking it is not admitted other utility than the utility of the self and consequently it reduces the utility to selfishness.

On this basis we explain the phenomenon of *Tangentopoli* that cannot be considered as an occasional statistical increase of political crime, but as a sign of the times. It is the projection of the great historic cultural disease of Hegelian Monism.

The instruments used for the establishment of the monstrous organic representation of the hedonistic moment of value are essentially the

1) Notes on the philosophy of value

constitutional states (both liberals and socialists), the central banks, the anonymous companies and the corporations.

Since the enjoyment of commodities takes place practically in the right of the property - which is precisely enjoyment of goods legally protected - capitalism has made the expropriation against people or by the constitutional norm of the socialist states in the capitalist state, or by the nominal currency (which is money-debt because it issued by central banks as a loan) in the usurocratic capitalism of liberal states, or by the provision of capital in anonymous companies in which the partner is transformed from owner to stockholder, i.e. creditor of junk debts equal to the whole capital vested in.

In all these legal cases, the common denominator is that the property becomes apparently a legal ghost, substantially in the instrumental societies: the nomenclature in the socialist states, the masonry in the liberal states, the union's majority stake (which has nothing to do with the majority of shareholders) in the corporation's board of directors: mainly banks and corporations.

On this basis we realise that the human community today lives in a system that has the prerogative of a breeding farming, and not that of the society of men.
This has been possible because it has achieved a strategy of domination by a culture based on ethics economist of Hegelian principles.

Only on this basis can it be explained why, contextually at the birth of the nominal money, banks were all conceived as instrumental subjectivity.
It was accomplished with the Bank of England (1694) the monstrous representation of an organic hedonistic moment of the value by transforming the people from owners into debtors of their own money because it incorporated and consolidated the rule to allow the

bank to issue currency only by lending it. When one considers that the sum of the monetary unit incorporates a value, that is a purchasing power equal to that of all the measured or measurable by the value, this value may assume either a mirror image duplicated or the positive sign of the ownership - and in this it doubles the wealth of nations - or the negative sign of debt that falls on people in an inescapable anguish insolvency. In fact, when the central bank issues money as a loan - as it is happen today - the money costs the 200% because it expropriates and puts the community into debt of their own money, moreover with the additional burden of interest.

Not surprisingly, the transformation of people from owners in debtors of their own money (through the replacement of the gold coin with the nominal money) occurred simultaneously with two instrumental subjectivity (based on the economist ethics of the money of *"to serve yourself"* instead of *"to serve"*): constitutional state and central bank.

2) Why the Euro is an awkward currency?

When the moneylender does something there is always a reason. Everyone understood, through a daily painful experience, that the Euro is an uncomfortable currency.
Only few people have understood the real reason. The majority of the public opinion believes that it is an inescapable necessity related to the replacement of the old with the new currency. It is a false belief because the numbers are, in this case, freely programmable. As usual the most difficult things to observe are the obvious ones, such as moustache, which is not seen because they are under the nose. The bearer of the Euro is like the bearer of a moustache.

In fact, the discomfort of the Euro is an incentive to use credit cards or debit cards which replaces *l'argent de poche*, i.e. currency from their own pockets, the commercial banks money.
With ATM our pocket turns into a real bank branch in which are calculated the costs of deposits and withdrawal services. In this way the banks make use of our pockets as the venue of its own agency, without paying rent and increasing control on an additional liquidity otherwise unattainable.

The Euro is like the number of the beast spoken by the Apocalypse, which is on the forehead and on the hand and that needs to buy and sell. It adds money to the current debt not due, further damage of spontaneous slavery towards the great usury.

3) The "colonial" currency

We have been saying it for years and now the facts have been proven: the Euro is a currency of Class B, because it operates in a disorderly market; the European market, in fact, lacks of energy sources. Only economists with no culture can consider the Euro a suitable currency to strengthen the prerogatives of sovereignty.
To give an example, today the Euro is like a factory that can produce all the goods except one; the Euro can buy everything except oil, and when Europe needs oil it has to use the dollar.

The history master of life has taught us that when Europe was completing the organicity of the market with the opening to the Eastern markets, America intervened in Kosovo with the ridiculous pretext of fighting smugglers of oil. That is why the Euro can only assume the feature of the colonial currency.

It has been more than five years since we said that the dollar would have disintegrated the Euro for two reasons: because it had interest in doing this, and because it has the strength to do this. The result of the monetary strategy, imposed to the European market by the top of the Federal Reserve Bank, was predicted by Giuseppe Palladino, who defined it as stagflation, which means economic stagnation and monetary undervaluation, now improperly indicated as inflation, which is when the amount of money in circulation is too large compared to the increases of production. Today, money is scarce and undervalued, so it has a double thrust into poverty, because money is less and worth less.

3) The "colonial" currency

The great money lenders have designed it in this way because they want to expropriate the people, indebtedness their money, moreover rarefy it by the usurocratic banking techniques.

Europe is under the sword of Damocles the great money-lender exactly like Argentina. The only response to this aggression of the great usury is the popular ownership of money, i.e. remove the ownership of currency from the Central Bank (a private company) and attribute it to the people upon issuance.

4) The outrageous falsehoods of scandals or the true scandal of falsehoods?

With the discovery of the induced value not only changes the reading of history but also of the financial statements.
The dramatic explosion of the huge scandals that touches the heads of majors economic world-scale complexes in America is, in our opinion, caused by the fact that all economic schools have not yet figured out what is the currency. The macroscopic result of this cultural disease is: or the pretension to deny the existence of money as an economic property (defining it, according to the theory of nihilism monetary, as "nothing" or "neutral instrument of exchange"), or to propose the definition as "debt and / or credit".

If the first hypothesis were true, we should be indifferent to have or to not have money in our pocket and thieves should be set free because they stole "nothing". If the second was real a debt of money would be "a debt of a debt".

While the first hypothesis was considered only by economists of the literary society, the second is, unfortunately, that it was considered by the drafters of the financial statements of central banks and multinational corporations because they are forced to admit, albeit incorrectly, that the currency exists.

An old farmer friend of mine, taught me that the worst fault of the louse is not to suck blood, but to be an idiot because he cannot do

4) The outrageous falsehoods of scandals or the true scandal of falsehoods?

anything else: and the idiot is more dangerous than a criminal because it is completely unpredictable.

Once proven that money is a real asset because it is not only the measure of the value, but also the value of the measure (because each unit of measure has necessarily the quality corresponding to what it has to measure: as the meter has the quality of the length because it measures the length, money has the quality of the value because it measures the value) all the U.S. Economic system is in deficit because there is no distinction between induced value and credit-value, i.e. between money and debt, all financial statements are fatally reported in debt also the value of the currency as it is conceived as a currency-debt that is the nominal money, or to use Ciampi's words (bill proposed by Ciampi's Government 10 February 1993) a *"junk debt"* (as to say *"thin air"*).

The American crisis could have been caused by a macroscopic falsification of the financial statements in which they are reported as a debt, i.e. as a negative value, the monetary values that are instead highly positive financial assets because that costs nothing (as products, as each unit of measure, by the simple mental activities of social convention), consolidated and funded in the purchasing power that mirror duplicates the value of all real properties measured or measurable in the value. In this way the currency-debt, instead of mirror duplicating the value of real assets, that is the wealth of American people, they precipitate in the anguish of inevitable insolvency, because at the moment of issuance, the cost of money is 200%, it transforms in "+ 100%" in "- 100%". The cultural diseases are the most deleterious.

As you can see, my farmer friend was right: the idiots (monetarist) are more dangerous than the delinquents, and the principle not only applies to America, but at global level too.

The Utopian Country

My advice to the President of the United States is, therefore, to review the budgets taking into account the distinction between money and debt (as if to say debt and the way to pay it). Also the Bank of Italy has always reported in its financial statements the currency issued as debt the money issued. To lend is a quality of the owner, not of the debtor.

You can fool some of the people all of the time, and all of the people some of the time, but you can not fool all of the people all of the time.

5) The reasons behind the "face off" between Industrial Confederation and the Unions. The malady of surplus value and flexibility

In the social categories misconceptions are like diseases of the human body and chronic diseases in the working world are two: the *surplus value* and *flexibility*.

When Marx said that the employer took advantage parasitically of the employer because he appropriated the profit margin, that is the surplus value, he laid the ideological premise on which the Labour Union was founded on as an instrument of revolution in order to claim, in the form of increased in wages, the surplus value.
Since free-labour differs from the slave-labour because it is based on free negotiation of compensations, the exaggerated application of the theory of surplus value, destroys the contract of employment, because it destroys the interest of the employer to contract. This cultural disease is the waiting room or for *"unemployment"* or for *"work without a contract"* (which is the return to slavery or at least undeclared work). With the advent of globalization and international competition in the labour markets, this disease has became so aggravated to explode into conflict not only between employers and unions, but also against government authorities.

The prognosis is very unfavourable with the second disease of flexibility, for which treatment is impossible because the diagnosis was wrong. With the flexibility, reducing the purchasing power of wages is not attributable to the employer or to the government, but at the top of the central banks because only they have the power to determined arbitrarily deflationary pressures or underestimation monetary forcing employers or cease productive activities, or to accept flexibility in adapting the cost and price to the oscillation of monetary values that lead the same globalization of markets.

So the union's demands with their complaints (including the so-called untouchable art. 18 [a]) should not be raised as a union conflict against employers, but against the Central Bank, in a compact way by the government, employers and workers. The flexibility relates in fact to the purchasing power of the money. The induced value has nothing to do with the surplus.

The radical solution of these problems (and not only them) is implementing the principle of popular ownership of the money. Only by returning the money to its rightful owners will be possible to rationalise the system. No coincidence if St. Thomas says that ethics is an aspect of rationality."

---

[a] Article 18 of Italy's labour code, which requires companies that employ 15 or more workers to re-hire (rather than compensate) any employee found to have been fired without just cause

6) The "snag" in art. 107 of the Maastricht Treaty. Europe like Argentina?

Yes! The validity of this diagnosis is based on two key issues:
1) Art. 107 of the Treaty of Maastricht;
2) The advent of the Euro.

At the first reading of the Treaty, even if unpleasantly surprised by Article 107, we did not understand the real why of the Treaty. Today, after the drama of Argentina, we finally understood.

Art. 107 - which prohibits any possible contact or interference between the Member States and the European Central Bank in the phase of issuance – it was officially justified on the principle of the need to protect the Euro from inflationary pressures or stresses. (This requirement could be satisfied on the basis of standard criteria for "technical discretion" well known to the schools of banking statistics, so much so that this rule has not precedents).

The truth is that they wanted to raise an impassable wall similar to that which separates the states from foreign central banks. In other words, with Art. 107 the relationship between European countries and the ECB is identical to that existing between Argentina and the U.S. Federal Reserve Bank. On this basis the issue of the Euro is made by the ECB as if it were a loan to a foreign state.

Apparently, as the central bank issues money only in lending it, it may seem that between the issuance of money at home or abroad there is no difference, as we well know - and better than us it is known by the drafters of Art. 107 - that the loan abroad is greatly demanded in return for normal and international custom, as made in favour of strangers; the domestic loan is attenuated and / or deferred for the contacts and the solicitations that normally characterize the relationship between central bank and government: these same contracts that the high bank lodge carefully would keep away as they are particularly troublesome to the moneylenders regime.

In other words, with Art. 107 and the advent of the Euro, Europe is in the same subordination as that of Argentina against the dollar.
Europe put herself in debt, in fact, for debts not due, however, in favour of the ECB, for a value equal to all banknotes in circulation, with no possibility to avoid the sword of Damocles of the debts (not due), falls, as in Argentina, on his head.

The very fact that in the Maastricht Treaty Art. 107 was promptly inserted in none suspicious times, it makes us think that the *"pro tempore Damocles"*, the governor Duysemberg, had serious intentions to let the sword fall, by imitating what his colleague, Alan Greenspan, had done, with Argentina.

So the "sword" exist and is there above our heads. We hope that it will not fall, but this hope is not enough.
That is why there should be an emergency-currency that allows money to fill the monetary gaps similar to those in Argentina. Money is like blood, its quantity must be adjusted to the size of the body to supply, and we must prepare for the transfusion, the availability, eliminating the risk of the deadly collapse. The Argentine government understood this truth and designed an alternative currency, the Argentinian, whose issuance was prevented, as is known, by the intervention of usurocratic and supranational authority.

Our advantage is the fact that - on the initiative by the Union Anti-usury Saus – an alternative currency has already been born in Italy,

6) The "snag" in art. 107 of the Maastricht Treaty. Europe like Argentina?

the SIMEC, which helps to cope in times of emergency because it was designed in a way that it cannot be controlled by the central bank because it was designed as ***"Ownership of the Bearer"*** and ***"without reserve"***, like gold, and obtained the chrism of legitimacy by the Order of the Court of Chieti (on 21 st September 2000, No. 127) and published on the Unified European Catalogue of the Italian currency (Alpha Edizioni, Torino, 2001, page 791, where it is officially quoted: "Current virtual value: 1000 Simec = 2000 Lira").

It is therefore necessary promotes the SIMEC-euro and/or Euro-SIMEC conversion by funds of convertibility made for this purpose, in conferring to the fund not the property, but only the availability for the exchange rate. In this way the shareholder of the fund, it will be the owner of both the Euro and the SIMEC.

7) Karl Marx was the first to denounce the giant scam. "Reducing taxes by eliminating the waste"???!!!

The waste must be erased as such and not to "reduce taxes".

On this essential introduction, we accept with enthusiasm the President Berlusconi's programme. Therefore, in the fundamental rule that before considering the straw it is better to deal with the beam, it must be said that the major and fundamental "fiscal waste" is the payment to the central bank of the debt not due for all the money in circulation.

The citizen, in good faith, thinks that the tax deduction is used to pay the costs required for public purposes.
Nothing could be different from the truth. As is well known and indisputable, most of the taxes goes into the pockets of the Central Bank's shareholders (limited private company with profit purpose) because the central bank issues money only to lend, and since lending money is a prerogative of the owner and the owner must be those who create the value of money - that is who accepts it and not who prints it - the amount due to the central bank should be commensurate to what is usually due to the printer. Therefore, here is the "fiscal waste" is equal to the difference between printing cost and nominal value of money.

It Could have a semblance of credibility to finalize the tax deduction for paying debts to the central bank, when the issuance was based on

7) Karl Marx was the first to denounce the giant scam. "Reducing taxes by eliminating the waste"???!!!

the monetary reserves (gold).
Since lending money is a prerogative of the owner, the bank could say, *"the money is mine because the reserves are mine, thus I can issue the money in lending it"*. With the end of the Bretton Woods Agreements on 15th August 1971 there was historical evidence, as well as a scientific one of the uselessness of the reserve, otherwise the dollar, that from that date, would totally lose its value because deprived of the reserve. Thus, the community creates the value of money because it accepts it and not the bank that issues it.

Upon issuance, conventionally it creates two different legal means: the *loan* and the *object of the loan*: debt and the *subject of debt*.
When the tax deduction is made to pay this debt, the taxpayer pays the bank to return its own money that instead should be credited to himself who, by accepting it, creates the value.

On this basis we explain the ridiculous definitions given by monetarists connected to the system such as: *"money is nothing"* **(16)** or *"junk debt"* **(17)** with the evident purpose of concealing the object of fraud by which the people have been transformed from owners (when the currency was gold) into debtors of its own currency (by the nominal money).

The first to denounce this gigantic scam was Karl Marx:
"At their birth the great banks, decorated with national titles, were only associations of private speculators, who placed themselves by the side of governments, and, thanks to the privileges they received, were in a position to advance money to the State. Hence the accumulation of the national debt has no more infallible measure than the successive rise in the stock of these banks, whose full development dates from the founding of the Bank of England in 1694. The Bank of England began with lending its money to the Government at 8%; at the same time it was empowered by

The Utopian Country

Parliament to coin money out of the same capital, by lending it again to the public in the form of banknotes. It was allowed to use these notes for discounting bills, making advances on commodities, and for buying the precious metals. It was not long ere this credit-money, made by the bank itself, became. the coin in which the Bank of England made its loans to the State, and paid, on account of the State, the interest on the public debt. It was not enough that the bank gave with one hand and took back more with the other; it remained, even whilst receiving, the eternal creditor of the nation down to the last shilling advanced." **(18)**.

This message of Marx was totally ignored by all governments, even by Marxists. If the Berlusconi Government will do what he said it would do, eliminating the debt caused by the fraud of monetary issue, he will write a new page of history. In fact, there is no "greater waste" than the tribute paid not only for a debt not due, but even for an own credit passed for debt. That is why **everybody can lend money except those who issue it**. The charity of banks are stronger than Christian ones: Christian charity teaches us to forgive debts, while the charity of banks has taught the debtor even to pay the central banks which collects as creditors their own debts.

If Mr. Berlusconi does not consider our message he will give evidence that it his intention to eliminate the waste of straws and not that of the beam.

---

(16) Massimo Fini, Money dung of the devil, Marsilio, Venice.
(17) Bill proposed by the Ciampi Government 10 February 1993, Acts of Parliament.
(18) C. Marx, Capital, Book I, chapter 31: *Genesis of the Industrial Capitalist*, paragraph 6, Editions, Moscow 1974, pp. 817-818.

8) Monetary strategy during the FIAT crisis

Mr. Umberto Agnelli, when speaking about the FIAT crisis, spoke about the participation of a "strategic quota".

Strategic choices have the essential quality of being simple. Strategy is a science in which the children's logic is applied.

To understand the true reason for the crisis in Turin it should first be pointed out that Fiat is in crisis due to lack of money. The insolvency of the debt is in fact caused by the inability to pay. At first sight this might seem like a joke. But no: this is the real crux of the problem.

When money was gold, the rarity of the coin was rigid and uncontrollable because it is based on "natural law" of the existence and availability of the metal. With the advent of the nominal money and the abolition of the "gold standard", the rarity is arbitrarily programmed with the fierce parsimony behind the doors of the great usurers of the central banks.

FIAT has never had liquidity problems when its union controlled the majority of the shares (called participants) of the Bank of Italy. With the advent of the Euro it became a drop in the bucket of the shareholders of the ECB, and since, with globalization, it is historically verified the proverb "it's the same the whole world over", because the world has become such the same, the mix of central banks has been largely unified in the same hands of real money masters, according to the masterful and prophetic definition of Marx: *"At their birth the great banks, decorated with national titles, were only associations of private speculators, who placed themselves by the side of governments, and, thanks to the privileges they received, were in a position to advance money to the State."* **(19)**

This means that the distinction between central banks should not be inferred from the "national denominations" but those of "speculators" who control them.

The "Ltd", instrumental subjectivity in which central banks constitute themselves, are the screens of the large manger because they allow the great usurers to secretly steal into anonymity (from which the exact title of "anonymous company") by transforming the people into debtors of their own money.

On this introduction it explains why the crisis of FIAT was the result of the Argentinian one, where important Italian banks have been bled by the decision of the Federal Reserve Bank that requested payment of debts due established on the issuance of dollars. All the people of the world are subjected to the sword of the "pro tempore Damocles" masters of central banks. Also Europe is in the same condition.

Therefore, it seems appropriate to close this short note with the words recalled by Ezra Pound: *"To say that a state cannot pursue its aims because there is no money, is like saying that an engineer cannot build roads because there are no kilometres."*

---

(19) C. Marx, Cit. op., pp.. 817-818.

9) "Descent of the Barbarians"

When the barbarian hordes moved in medieval Europe they were using lances, clubs, arrows, fire and stones.

With the French Revolution, the barbarian hordes of the great usurers, led by the Bank of England (defined by Ezra Pound "Liberal usurers"), have replaced the weapons with the traditional slogans of ideologies. The formula for supporting all popular protests, *"Liberty, Equality, Fraternity"*, was invented, they say, by an English banker.

Since then until now nothing has changed.

A few days ago on the television a slogan was launched: "land rights", shouted by a crowd of immigrants. If we consider that the Kurds, people without a land, were transported to Italy at a cost of ten million each (equal to Euro 2,582.28) paid by the owners of central banks, traditionally transporters of human cattle as slave traders, we begin to realise that this slogan is the weapon conceived by the bankers, to establish between the Kurdish people and the Italian the same incompatibility report between Palestinians and Israelis.

The Barbarian hordes of money-lenders have invaded the world using sophisticated and perfidious weapons of slogans as strategies of domination based on aberrant psychological stress. Much more damaging because of the strike of the sword is the guilt complex caused by the charge of "racism" challenged with the deafening clamour of the media for who want to oppose the invasion of herds

The Utopian Country

of non-EU immigrants.
The right to have land is a sacred right, on condition that it is freed from seigniorage usury. Every population is in fact recognized as owner of his land on condition that he is owner and not a debtor, of his currency in his home.

Money for men is like water for fish. In times of drought, the fish leaves the arid areas to go to the puddled of water. On this rule, the bankers of the 18 th century, called by Pound the century of usury, have moved millions of men from Europe to America, creating monetary rarity in Europe and plenty of money in America. The great money-lenders have applied to the herds of non-EU immigrants the same rule.

That is why, for an absolute imperative historical necessity, every population needs to be the owner of its currency. Naturally for every non-EU immigrant their interest is to return to his land, to have his own currency, using the "law of water and fish," in opposite direction to that of the usurer.

To make every population the **owner of his money** is much more than a slogan: it is a strong idea, possible to write new history pages. To pass through the age of usury (born in 1694 with the currency debt of the Bank of England) to that of civilization. This is the charismatic mission of our generation.

10) The chain letter and the sword of Damocles in the hands of the great usurers

It is characteristic of the human soul to anticipate at the present the expected values. That is why the mercantile practice of using the promissory note not only as a promise to pay, but also as a medium of payment, was born. With the promissory note, the prediction of fulfilment is enhanced by "legal certainty" as the debtor may be forced to pay by law.

If the debtor pays the promissory note regularly, all obligatory relations established among the endorsers and the endorsed are satisfied. If it is not paid, the insolvency bounces relentlessly on all related parties as endorsers of the bill in circulation. This is how was born the scam of the chain letter and explains why the protest for bills of exchange of the insolvent debtor is considered by the legislature with particular severity, because it affects the expectation in the monetary circulation.

The most serious form of chain letter is the monetary issuance. The nominal money was born as a promissory note issued by the central bank governor (that is the formula *"I promise to pay the bearer on demand the sum of"* signed: The Governor of the Bank of England), not as a "citizen" but as a "connection in a higher rank".
In fact, while the citizen, if he fails to pay, is liable for insolvency with the loss of dignity in the legal status of "protest bills of exchange", the governor not only issues a bill with no guarantee of

payment, even if he signed as a borrower - he issues it as a loan, that is, as a creditor.
The object of this loan would be a junk debt of the banker, who is, therefore, the real creditor and false debtor of real money masqueraded as a false bill.

When the issuance of currency was based on the reserve, money could be considered as a promissory note, conceived as a document of title, representative of the reserve.
The banker could well say: *"Money is mine because the reserve is mine."* Abolished the reserve, with the end of Bretton Woods Agreement, finally you have the historical evidence that the monetary value is purely conventional, like a rare stamp.

Money has a value simply because we agreed that it has.
Therefore, money must be ownership of who accepts it and not who issues it: it must be of the people and not of the bank. When lending the money, the banker at that moment hangs to the chain letter the sword of Damocles that is in the condition, or to give to every people its own money and renew the loan in making money also from the interests, or to drop the sword of Damocles by requiring the payment of debts not due, as the Federal Reserve Bank did with Argentina.

Unless we recover the ownership of our money, the whole world will continue to live under the sword of Damocles hanging on to the chain letter, which hangs from the hands of the giants of crime of the great usury.

11) Money as blood

As the blood distributes oxygen throughout the body, so does money distribute the purchasing power to the market. This basic principle has not been understood by the stupidity of the monetarists, because while the object picked up and carried by the red blood cell is known exactly as *"oxygen"*, up until now it was missing the definition of *monetary oxygen*: the **induced value** which is the **purchasing power** that is, the prediction given to the bearer of currency as a pure conventional value.

This fundamental and serious cultural gap is based on ignorance of the same concept of value. The value is always an estimation, i.e. a dimension of time and not of space, a spiritual reality and not goods. The currency, albeit with a symbol that costs nothing, has value because it gives to the bearer the expectation that it can buy.

The category of monetary values has made the cultural monopoly of the initiation school of big money lenders of the central banks, while to the "human cattle" was reserved the teaching of two hypotheses:
a) monetary nihilism (for which money is nothing and the only real value is the object of exchange);
b) the currency-debt of bearer, to say nominal money (of which the bank is the owner and, for this is issues that loans).

The common denominator of these two choices is the threat of death of the market; in the first case by asphyxiation because it is denied the very existence of monetary oxygen; in the second case by poisoning because the bearer is conceived not as owner but as a debtor of his own money.

On these aberrant theories dominates the hegemony of the usurer who can safely rob the population after having convinced them that or the stolen object has no value, or that they have to accept at the moment of its issuance the money as debt not due that is as a loan.

On this basis we can understand not only the difference between nominal money-debt of the bearer and money- gold properties of the bearer, but also between two different conceptions of life, between British Commonwealth and the Holy Roman Empire, between barbarism and civilization, between the ethics of instrumental economist subjectivity for which social function operates on the rule of *"to serve yourself"* (not for surprisingly all banks in the world are legal ghosts – Ltd) and natural ethics of organic society (made up of living people) based on the rule of *"to serve"*.

Only after having clarified that monetary oxygen is the purchasing power of money (that is the value of money created by social convention) as in the bloodstream blood cells carry oxygen into the capillaries, so money is distributed recognizing to each person the right to its share of citizen's income, as the owner and not as a debtor of its own currency.

The pockets of the citizens are the capillaries of the monetary system. Rightly it reminds us the heretics economists that the best place to store money are the pockets of the people **(20)**.
We are breathing the poisoned air of the currency-debt issued since 1694, by Bank of England, and the banks all over the world are following their example.

With the advent of globalization, we already feel the first signs of the monetary war which is the prelude to death.
That is why it is necessary to prevent it with a global reform for a

11) Money as blood

true and definite monetary justice.

Each single currency - whatever the state or the central bank that issues it - must declare, for the international convention, the ownership of the bearer and without reserve.

The only currency accepted, up to date conventionally by all states of the world was gold. If you want to establish a new universal currency, we must imitate the gold. To date, this it was not possible because there were no cultural basis for doing this.

This currency, based (like the SIMEC) on the new discovery of the induced value, must have the same positive qualities as gold: **ownership of the bearer** and **without reserve**, and not those of high negative production costs and exasperated and uncontrollable rarity. Since the price is not only the index of the value of commodities, but also the point of market saturation, the market needs to be considered saturated, both of commodity than of money, only when prices tend to coincide with the cost of production. This is the real law of monetary rarity that needs to be institutionalized in an international convention to free people from arbitrary rarefaction of money and real assets.

If money is the blood of the market, there must be neither too much money or too little, otherwise we would have monetary imbalances, the same diseases such as anaemia or hyperaemia. Since the monetary function is a constitutive element, essential for the political sovereignty, it needs be reminded the following anecdote.

When Machiavelli was asked what was the most important quality of a prince, he said: "The sense of measure". That is why the money lenders cannot be a prince. The sense of measure is incompatible with the fierce parsimony on which has been programmed the central bank and the money-debt, the nominal money that has turned people into owners to debtors of the monetary values.

We have been patient 308 years. Enough is enough! The revenge of blood against the gold of usurocracy is a new page of history for future generations.

A radical and definitive monetary restoration is necessary so that finally we can again breath clean monetary oxygen, purified from the venom of the debt due to the big seigniorage usury.

---

(20) *"The safest place to store money is in the people's trousers"*, E. Pound, Labour and usury, p. 72.

12) The Euro as strong as the "Quota 90" Lira?

Alberto De Stefani - who was Minister of Treasury and Finance of the first fascist government, Professor of Economics and Public Finance in the Faculty of Political Science at the University "La Sapienza" of Rome – said:
"Mussolini has lost the war with the "quota 90".

I learned that the "quota 90" was the process by which the lira was revalued against the pound of 25%: the ratio for the pound was reduced from 120 to 90 Lira.
Mussolini enthusiastically accepted the project because the advisers of the Bank of Italy (Stringer, Paratore, Beneduce and Volpi di Misurata) proposed as a sign of prestige and enhancing of dignity of the Italian State at international level. *"Stronger Lira"* meant, for Mussolini, *"stronger Italy"*, just like today, for Duysenberg and Prodi, *"stronger Euro"* means *"stronger Europe"*.

De Stefani made me realize that, with an inflation adjustment of 25%, would equally increase loans and debts. Banks were enriched and businesses failed for the unjustified and unpredictable complication of debts incurred to finance productive activities.

Italy went to war unarmed due to failures caused by the inevitable insolvency as a result of an unjustified increase in the value of money subject to debt.

Nothing new under the sun. With the revaluation of the Euro, everyone praised the strong currency, just as Mussolini did with the quota 90.
On this basis you can understand why America has closed its steel imports from Europe.

Since the price of steel was to compensate mainly for the payment of oil, Europe today finds itself, not only in the position that it cannot pay for oil, but also with further complications of its debt, caused by the blockage of exports and the revaluation of the Euro.

There is only one way to free from the slavery of usury: **the popular ownership of money**. Every population needs to be the master of their own currency at the moment of issuance, meaning depriving the central bank of the hegemony of seigniorage, in a fully democratic regime in which each population has in addition to political sovereignty, also the monetary one.

Carthago Delenda est.

12) The Euro as strong as the "Quota 90" Lira?

THE SOLUTION

BILL PROPOSAL for the "Popular Ownership of Money"

11th January 1995

The Utopian Country

13) Bill for the popular ownership of the Euro

HONOURABLE MEMBERS OF THE PARLIAMENT!
The purpose of this proposal is to fill a legislative gap no longer tolerable, already reported, moreover, by the bill *"Popular Ownership of Money"*
(Senate XII Legislature, No 1282, communication of the President on 11 January 1995) initiative of Senator Natali and others, and then (XIII Legislature Senate, No. 1288), initiative of Senator Monteleone and others.

No rule states, in fact, to who should be the owner of the Euro at the time of its original acceptance.

The truth is that money has value because it is the *measurement of value* and also, necessarily, the *value of the measure*. Each unit of measure has, in fact, the quality corresponding to what should be measured: as the meter has the quality of the length because it measures the length, the currency has the quality of value because it measures the value. Therefore, the currency symbol is not only the formal manifestation of the monetary agreement, but also the container of the value induced and incorporated into the symbol that is precisely the value of the measure, that is the purchasing power.
With the discovery of induced value as a pure legal value (see G. Auriti, *"The International Ordering of the Monetary System"*, Edigrafital, Teramo, 1993, p. 43 et seq.) it has finally given scientific justification of the monetary value.

As it has been demonstrated, a similar case occurs of physical induction. As the dynamo turns mechanical energy into an electrical one, so money transforms the value of the agreement, i.e. a legal instrument in a real commodity, object of the right of ownership: money.

In short, the value of money is caused not by the body of issuance – who by preparing and delivering the symbols, determines only the formal assumption of the monetary value – but by the acceptance of the community. The issue of symbols in conformity with the legal tender (the forced system) is an act of *"heteronomy";* the acceptance of money, which determines the conventional value, is an act of *"autonomy".*

The value of the Euro was born and persists in its continuity because conventionally accepted as a measure of value and measured value as subject of exchange. For these reasons, the Euro is, and can only be owned by the bearer who, with his behaviour, causes and helps to preserve its value.

The Maastricht Treaty is appropriately limited to the first stage to consider the issue, ignores all of the creative moment of monetary value, so much so that no provision of the Treaty considers who is the right owner of the Euro and how it should be attributed. Particularly significant is the content declared on the symbol affixed by the body of issuance. It appears only the word "Euro" preceded by numeric expression and subscription under the name of the Governor, in various languages, of the European Central Bank with the year of issuance. It is obvious, in this respect, the clear difference with the currencies of the other Member States, who traditionally conceived the money as a title representative of the credit claim for the reserve. The central bank was, in fact, considered as the owner of the value of money because it was considered owner of the value of the reserves, as such entitled to issue loans because "to lend" is the

13) Bill for the popular ownership of the Euro

prerogative of the owner.

With the end of the Bretton Woods Agreements (15th August 1971), the monetary reserve was abolished, and the replacement of the conventional value to that credit is evident. This explains the *"silence"* as *"object"* of the securities declaration on the Euro notes, since it is not possible to justify any more the issuance by loan because of lack of justification (even absurd) of the reserve, and banks rely on the mere practice consolidated in parasitic seigniorage, traditional of the central bank. Once, in fact, demonstrated that who creates the value of money is not who issues it, but who accepts it, lending means imposing a cost on the issuance of money by 200%.
When you equate the two phases of the issuing and acceptance, resulting in a serious injustice in legal regime of monetary values.
This has historically occurred with the advent of the nominal currency system of the central banks.

Once, those who found a gold nugget, appropriated it without becoming a debtor towards the mine. Today, instead of the mine there is the central bank, instead of the nugget of gold there is a piece of paper, instead of the property a debt, because the bank loans only money, while those who create the value is one who accepts it.
The merely instrumental moment of the issue of symbols has invaded that of the hedonistic one of the ***ownership of money***, so that the central bank, issuing currency by lending, expropriates and puts in debt the collectivity of his own money without a counterpart. That is ***why anyone can lend money except those who issue it***.
Levering on the conditioned reflex caused by the secular habit of always giving a valuable consideration to money, central banks, confusing the phase of issue with that of the circulation, led all the people of the world to accept its own currency, on the issue, with the amount of debt, that is by loan. By replacing the gold coin with the nominal money, people were so transformed from owners to debtor of their own money in the biggest scam of all time, going unnoticed

because too obvious. This originated in 1694 with the issuance of the sterling and the constitution of the Bank of England.

Today, with the advent of the Euro, Europe is in the privileged position of being able to replace currency-debt owned by the central bank, with its own currency.
Nothing in the Treaty of Maastricht considers, in fact, to who should the ownership of the Euro be. This is proof that the Treaty only considers the issuance and ignores the phase of acceptance. (Probably this was because it relied on the possibility to continue the practice of the monstrous "usurocratic Seigniorage", for which the European people should borrow, without compensation towards the ECB for a value equal the whole Euro currency in circulation.)

This means that the exclusive jurisdiction of the European People is left to regulate independently the regime of the acceptance of money and of the ownership, on which the ECB has not power to interfere like the Member States has not power to interfere in the issuance phase pursuant to art. 107 of the Treaty of Maastricht.

Because *"qui tacet neque adfirmat neque negat"*, it is clear that the EBC, for the limit imposed by the unique and essential meaning of the word "acceptance" as an exclusive competence of those who agrees, and not of who issues, cannot do more than take application of the principle that ownership of the Euro was created for the explicit recognition of the standard conventional law, as property of the European population for the only fact that, by accepting it, they create the value.

The acceptance of the Euro as the ownership of the bearer, leads to the award of two additional important purposes:
1) use the currency as an instrument of social law in implementation of the 2nd comma of art. 42 of the Constitution that stipulates the access to the property for all creating a right for the person with

13) Bill for the popular ownership of the Euro

content assets, such as citizen's income right;
2) rationalize the tax system by allowing the State to retain what is necessary for the needs of public utilities, eliminating costs and working time merely accountant and unproductive and the risks of tax evasion.

Given the imminence of the circulation of the Euro it is asked that this bill is put into question as a matter of urgency.

THE BILL

Article 1

- The Euro, on acceptance, born as ownership of citizens and shall be acquired for this purpose, for the availability of the Member States agreeing to the Treaty of Maastricht. The Euro is therefore property of the bearer.

Article 2

– To every citizen a code of social income is given, by which he is credited to the share of income caused by the monetary acceptance and other possible sources of income in the implementation of the 2 nd comma art. 42 of the Constitution.

Article 3

- Accepted the ownership of the Euro by representing the national community, the Government is entitled to retain at its origin, what is necessary for the needs of public utility tax.

Article 4

- Transitional Rule. It is granted a moratorium of debt on request of the parties, pending to assure who is the ownership of the Euro upon issuance.

Post Scriptum: Guardiagrele the Utopian Country

Marino Solfanelli, on whose shoulders is the responsibility for the publication of this short essay, has provoked in us to justify why Ezra Pound declared himself fascist. The need for this distinction arises from the fact that in *communis opino* (common opinion), this gesture of Pound is judged as a confession of a sin.

The cultural plagiarism programmed by the *winners* has in fact succeeded to pretend a fault as an advantage.
Because in politics what is not expressed does not exist (and expression has a cost) who paid the piper of history, has chosen the music of "false truth": The usurers, the money masters, have authoritatively and officially passed *usurocracy* for *democracy*.

If for democracy we mean the people sovereign, then the people must not only have the political sovereignty, but also the monetary sovereignty in a full democracy based on the "*thirst for justice*" (like the Roman plebiscite) and not the law of the number that is finalistically and ethically neutral. The experience has in fact taught us that frequently the political majority is achieved, not by those who love the people, but by those who have the money to buy it.

The word "*democracy*" was born seven centuries before in Greece, and not once had been used in the Gospel. The only time it is applied, the people put Christ on the cross and sends Barabbas free thus, according to democratic ethic, we should praise Barabbas and condemn Christ.

The Utopian Country

Democracy is, at its best, a code of procedure, not a code of honour

Pound understood that, when Mussolini declared and promoted *war of blood against gold*, he was absolutely right. He deeply felt this message of justice that he declared himself *fascist* with a moral and superhuman strength, recognizing as an American citizen, in time of war, his country was fighting on the wrong side. Fate had given him the land where he was born, but when he could personally chose where to live and die, he preferred the land, that was yes defeated, but on the side of blood rather than staying in a winning country, on the side of gold.

In a precious and prophetic note he says: *"On September 10th last year I passed along the Salaria Route, over Fara Sabina City, and after some time I entered the Republic of Utopia, a placid country lying off the present geography"* **(13)** and then he adds: "I had written:
"Utopia, a peaceful town lying eighty years East of Fara Sabina"(...) **(14)**.

The reader should not be shocked if we dare to think that the country of Utopia, prophesied by Pound, is the village of Guardiagrele.
Which is in fact East of the town Fara Sabina and in the same town, eighty years later, not by chance the *Poundian currency was born, property of the bearer and not of the bank, without debt and without reserve: the Simec.*

The war of blood against gold inevitably continues and we do not want to continue loosing. When the banker Lord Bennett says to Pound: *"It took twenty years to beat Napoleon, five years will be sufficient to defeat fascism"*, he showed his cultural superiority (not a moral one) because history has proved him right. Mussolini could not win the war because he did not understand that the enemy to beat was the gold of lenders: the money-debt of the Bank of England.

The *popular ownership of money* is the great revenge to the game of history that we faithfully associate to the heroes of every political stripe or grid, which fought on the same frontier, against usury.

We will transform all the nations of the world from debtors to owners of money, for the mere fact that this idea was born.

Sociologists say than the force of ideas that changed history, must have the *quality of novelty and simplicity*; this has also the one of the truth. And the ideas are affirmed with a proportional speed to their historical necessity.
That is why we are "*resigned*" to win... because, obviously, we can not lose.
This is, therefore, our prophetic utopia **(15)**.

---

(13) E. Pound, Labour and usury, p. 7.
(14) E. Pound, Labour and usury, p. 7, note 1.
(15) In the science field Utopia does not exist. If about a century ago someone said that we would have gone on the moon, they would have been taken for a madman.
We realize that transforming people from debtors in owners of their money is much more "utopian" than going to the moon.
After the discovery of the induced value of money as a phenomenon related to the science of law, the implementation of the popular ownership of money is not only possible but due to eliminate the seigniorage of the great usury.

The Utopian Country

www.ingramcontent.com/pod-product-compliance
Lightning Source LLC
Chambersburg PA
CBHW070426180526
45158CB00017B/845